Edith Wharton
The Vice of Reading

ERIS
gems

THAT "DIFFUSION OF KNOWLEDGE" commonly classed with steam-heat and universal suffrage in the category of modern improvements, has incidentally brought about the production of a new vice—the vice of reading.

No vices are so hard to eradicate as those which are popularly regarded as virtues. Among these the vice of reading is foremost. That reading trash is a vice is generally conceded; but reading *per se*— the habit of reading—new as it is, already ranks with such seasoned virtues as thrift, sobriety, early rising and regular exercise. There is, indeed, something peculiarly aggressive in the virtuousness of the sense-of-duty reader. By those who have kept to the humble paths of precept he is revered as following a counsel of perfection. "I wish I had kept up my reading as you have," the unlettered novice declares to this adept in the supererogatory; and the reader, accustomed to the incense of uncritical applause, not unnaturally looks on his occupation as a noteworthy intellectual achievement.

Reading deliberately undertaken—what may be called volitional reading—is no more reading than erudition is culture. Real reading is reflex action; the born reader reads as unconsciously as he breathes; and, to carry the analogy a degree farther, reading is no more a virtue than breathing. Just in proportion as it is considered meritorious does it become unprofitable. What is reading, in the last analysis, but an interchange of thought between writer and reader? If the book enters the reader's mind just as it left the writer's—without any of the additions and modifications inevitably produced by contact with a new body of thought—it has been read to no purpose. In such cases, of course, the reader is not always to blame. There are books that are always the same—incapable of modifying or of being modified—but these do not count as factors in literature. The value of books is proportionate to what may be called their plasticity—their quality of being all things to all men, of being diversely moulded by the impact of fresh forms of thought. Where, from one cause or the other, this reciprocal adaptability is lacking, there can be no real intercourse between book and reader. In this sense it may be said that there is no abstract standard of values in literature: the greatest books ever written are worth to each reader only what he can get out of them. The best books are those from which the best readers have been able to extract the greatest amount of thought of the highest quality; but it is generally from these books that the poor reader gets least.

To be a poor reader may therefore be considered a misfortune; but it is certainly not a fault. Why should we all be readers? We are not all expected to be musicians; but read we must; and so those that cannot read creatively read mechanically—as though a man who had no aptitude for the violin were to regard the grinding of a barrel-organ as an equivalent accomplishment! It must be understood at the outset that, in the matter of reading, the real offenders are not those who restrict themselves to recognized trash. There is little harm in the self-confessed devourer of foolish fiction. He who feasts upon "the novel of the day" does not seriously impede the development of literature. The cast of mind which discerns in the natural divisions of the melon an indication that it is meant to be eaten *en famille*, might even look upon certain works—the penny-in-the-slot or touch-the-button books, which require no effort beyond turning the pages and using one's eyes—as especially designed for the consumption of the mechanical reader. Providence turns out an unfailing supply of authors whose obvious mission it is thus to protect literature from the ravages of the unintelligent; and it is only when he strays from his predestined pastures that the mechanical reader becomes a danger to the body of letters. The idea that reading is a moral quality has unhappily led many conscientious persons to renounce their innocuous dalliance with light literature for more strenuous intercourse. These are the persons who "make it a rule to read". The "platform" of the more ambitious actually includes the large resolve to keep up with all that is being written! The desire to keep up is apparently the strongest incentive to this class of readers: they seem to regard literature as a cable-car that can be "boarded" only by running; while many a born reader may be found unblushingly loitering in the tea-cup times of stage-coach and posting-chaise, without so much as being aware of the new means of locomotion.

It is when the mechanical reader, armed with this high conception of his duty, invades the domain of letters—discusses, criticises, condemns, or, worse still, praises—that the vice of reading becomes a menace to literature. Even so, it might seem in questionable taste to resent an intrusion prompted by motives so respectable, were it not that the incorrigible self-sufficiency of the mechanical reader makes him a fair object of attack.

The man who grinds the barrel-organ does not challenge comparison with Paderewski, but the mechanical reader never doubts his intellectual competency. As grace gives faith, so zeal for self-improvement is supposed to confer brains.

To read is not a virtue; but to read well is an art, and an art that only the born reader can acquire. The gift of reading is no exception to the rule that all natural gifts need to be cultivated by practice and discipline; but unless the innate aptitude exist the training will be wasted. It is the delusion of the mechanical reader to think that intentions may take the place of aptitude.

So far is this from being the case that there are certain generic signs by which the born reader detects his manufactured copy under whatever guise the latter may assume. One of these idiosyncrasies is the habit of regarding reading objectively. The mechanical reader, as he always reads consciously, knows exactly how much he reads, and will tell you so with the pride of the careful housekeeper who has calculated to within half an ounce the daily consumption of food in her household. As the housekeeper is apt to go to market every day at a certain hour, so the mechanical reader has often a fixed time for laying in his intellectual stores; and not infrequently he reads for just so many hours a day. The statement in one of Hamerton's youthful diaries—"I shall now commence a course of poetical reading, beginning with 50 hours of Chaucer, and as I gave him 1½ last night it leaves me exactly 48½"—is a good example of this kind of reading. It follows that he who reads by time often "has no time to read"; a plight unknown to the born reader, whose reading forms a continuous undercurrent to all his other occupations.

The mechanical reader is the slave of his book-mark: if he lose his place he is under the irksome necessity of beginning again at the beginning; and a story is told of one such reader whom a flippant relative kept for a year at *Fire and Sword in the Soudan* by the unfeeling stratagem of shifting the marker every night. The born reader is his own book-mark. He instinctively remembers at what stage in the argument he laid his book down, and the pages open of themselves at the point for which he is looking. It is due to the mechanical reader to say that he is uniformly scrupulous in the performance of his task: it is one of his rules *never to skip a word*, and he can always meet with a triumphant affirmative Dr. Johnson's immortal "Do *you* read books *through?*" This inexorable principle is doubtless based on the fact that the mechanical reader is incapable of discerning intuitively whether a book is worth reading or not. In fact, until he has read the last line of a book he is unable to form any opinion of it; nor can he give any adequate reasons for his opinion when formed. Viewing all books from the outside, and having no point of contact with the author's mind, he makes no allowances for temperament or environment; for that process of transposition and selection that makes the most impersonal book the product of unique conditions.

It is obvious that the mechanical reader, taking each book separately as an entity suspended in the inane, must miss all the by-paths and cross-cuts of his subject. He is like a tourist who drives from one "sight" to another without looking at anything that is not set down in Baedeker. Of the delights of intellectual vagrancy, of the improvised chase after a fleeting allusion, suggested sometimes by the turn of a phrase or by the mere complexion of a word, he is serenely unaware. With him the book's the thing: the idea of using it as the keynote of unpremeditated harmonies, as the gateway into some *paysage choisi* of the spirit, is beyond his ken.

The mechanical reader considers it his duty to read every book that is talked about; a duty rendered less onerous by the fact that he can judge beforehand, from the material dimensions of each book, how much space it will take up in his head: there is no need to allow for expansion. To the mechanical reader, books once read are not like growing things that strike root and intertwine branches, but like fossils ticketed and put away in the drawers of a geologist's cabinet; or rather, like prisoners condemned to life-long solitary confinement. In such a mind the books never talk to each other.

The course of the mechanical reader is guided by the *vox populi*. He makes straight for the book that is being talked about, and his sense of its importance is in proportion to the number of editions exhausted before publication, since he has no means of distinguishing between the different classes of books talked about, nor between the voices that do the talking.

It is a part of the whole duty of the mechanical reader to pronounce an opinion on every book he reads, and he is sometimes driven to strange shifts in the conscientious performance of this task. It is his nature to mistrust and dislike every book he does not understand. "I cannot read and therefore wish all books burned." In his heart of hearts the mechanical reader may sometimes times echo this wish of Envy in *Doctor Faustus*; but, it being also a part of his duty to be "fond of reading", he is obliged to repress his bibliocidal impulse, and go through the form of trying the case, when lynching would have been so much simpler.

It is only natural that the reader who looks on reading as a moral obligation should confound moral and intellectual jugments. Here is a book that every one is talking about; the number of its editions is an almost unanswerable proof of its merit; but to the mechanical reader it is cryptic, and he takes refuge in disapproval. He admits the cleverness, of course; but one of the characters is "not nice"; *ergo,* the book is not nice; he is surprised that you should have cared to read it. The mechanical reader, after a few such experiments, learns the potency of disapproval as a critical weapon, and it soon becomes his chief defence against the irritating demand to admire

13

what he cannot understand. Sometimes his disapprobation is tempered by philosophic concessions to human laxity: as in the case of the lady who could not approve of Balzac's novels, but was of course willing to admit that "they were written in the most beautiful French". A fine instance of this temperate disapproval is furnished by Mrs Barbauld's verdict upon "The Ancient Mariner": she "pronounced it improbable".

The obligation of expressing an opinion on every book which is being talked about has led to the reprehensible but natural habit of borrowing opinions. Any one who frequents a group of mechanical readers soon becomes accustomed to their socialistic use of certain formulas, and to the rapid process of erosion and distortion undergone by much-borrowed opinions. There have been known persons heartless enough to find pleasure in taking the mechanical reader unawares with the demand for an opinion; and it must be owned that the result sometimes justifies the theory that no sports are so diverting as those which are seasoned with cruelty. In such extremities, the expedients resorted to by mechanical readers often do justice to their inventiveness; as when a lady, on being suddenly asked what she thought of *Quo Vadis*, replied that she had no fault to find with the book except that "nothing happened in it".

Thus far the subject has dealt only with what may be called the average mechanical reader: a designation embracing the immense majority of book-consumers. There is, however, another and more striking type of mechanical reader—he who, wearying of the Philistine diversion of "understanding the obvious", boldly threads his way "amid the bitterness of things occult". Transcendentalism owes much of its perennial popularity to a reverence for the unintelligible, and its disciples are largely recruited from the class of readers who consider it as great an intellectual feat to read a book as to understand it. But these votaries of the esoteric are too few in number to be harmful. It is the average mechanical reader who really endangers the integrity of letters; this may seem a curious charge to bring against that voracious majority. How can those who create the demand for the hundredth thousand be accused of malice toward letters?

In that acute character-study, *Manoeuvring*, Miss Edgeworth says of one of her characters: "Her mind had never been overwhelmed by a torrent of wasteful learning. That the stream of literature had passed over it was apparent only from its fertility." There could hardly be a happier description of those who read intuitively; and its antithesis as fitly portrays the mechanical reader. His mind is devastated by that torrent of wasteful learning which his demands have helped to swell. It is probable that if no one read but those who know how to read, none would produce books but those who know how to write; but it is the least offence of the mechanical reader to have encouraged the mechanical author. The two were made for each other and may prey on one another with impunity.

The harmfulness of the mechanical reader is fourfold. In the first place, by bringing about the demand for mediocre writing, he facilitates the career of the mediocre author. The crime of luring creative talent into the ranks of mechanical production is in fact the gravest offence of the mechanical reader.

Secondly, by his passion for "popular" renderings of abstruse and difficult subjects, by confounding the hastiest *réchauffé* of scientific truisms with the slowly-matured conceptions of the original thinker, he retards true culture and lessens the possible amount of really abiding work.

The habit of confusing moral and intellectual judgments is the third cause of his harmfulness to literature. The inadequacy of "art for art's sake" as a literary creed has long been conceded. It is not by requiring that the imaginative writer shall be touched "to fine issues" that the mechanical reader interferes with the production of masterpieces, but by his own inability to discern the "fine issues" of any book, however great, which presents some incidental stumbling-block to his vision. To those who regard literature as a criticism of life, nothing is more puzzling than this incapacity to distinguish between the general tendency of a book—its technical and imaginative value as a whole—and its merely episodical features. That the mechanical reader should confound the unmoral with the immoral is perhaps natural; he may be pardoned for an erroneous classification of such books as *La Chartreuse de Parme* or the *Life of Benvenuto Cellini*; his harmfulness to literature lies in his persistent ignorance of the fact that any serious portrayal of life must be judged not by the incidents it presents but by author's sense of their significance. The harmful book is the trivial book: it depends on the writer, and not on the subject, whether the contemplation of life results in Faust or Faublas. To gauge the absence of this perception in the average reader, one must turn to the ordinary "improper" book of current English and American fiction. In these works, enjoyed under protest, with the plea that they are "unpleasant, but so powerful", one sees the reflection of the image which the great portrayals of life leave on the minds of the mechanical reader and his novelist. There is the collocation of "painful" incidents; but the rest, being unperceived, is left out.

Finally, the mechanical reader, by his demand for peptonized literature, and his inability to distinguish between the means and the end, has misdirected the tendencies of criticism, or rather, has produced a creature in his own image—the mechanical critic. The London correspondent of a New York paper recently quoted "a well-known English reviewer" as saying that people no longer had time to read critical analyses of books—that what they wanted was a *résumé* of the contents. It is of course an open question (and one hardly within the scope of this argument) how much literature is benefited by criticism; but to speak as though the analysis of a book were one kind of criticism and the cataloguing of its contents another, is a manifest absurdity. The born reader may or may not wish to hear what the critics have to say of a book; but if he cares for any criticism he wants the only kind worthy of the name—an analysis of subject and manner. He who has no time for such criticism will certainly spare none to the summing-up of the contents of a book: an inventory of its incidents, ending up with the conventional "But we will not spoil the reader's enjoyment by revealing, etc." It is the mechanical reader who demands such inventories and calls them criticisms; and it is because the mechanical reader is in the majority that the mechanical plot-extractor is fast superseding the critic. Whether real criticism be of service to literature or not, it is clear that this pseudo-reviewing is harmful, since it places books of very different qualities on the same dead level of mediocrity, by ignoring their true purport and significance. It is impossible to give an idea of the value of any book, except perhaps a detective-story, by the recapitulation of its contents; and even those qualities which differentiate the good from the bad detective-story lie not so much in the collocation of incidents as in the handling of the subject and the choice of means used for producing a given effect. All forms of art are based on the principle of selection, and where that principle is held of no account in the sum-total of any intellectual production, there can be no genuine criticism.

It is thus that the mechanical reader systematically works against the best in literature. Obviously, it is to the writer that he is most harmful. The broad way that leads to his approval is so easy to tread and so thronged with prosperous fellow-travellers that many a young pilgrim has been drawn into it by the mere craving for companionship; and perhaps it is not until the journey's end, when he reaches the Palace of Platitudes and sits down to a feast of indiscriminate praise, with the scribblers he

has most despised helping themselves unre-
proved out of the very dish prepared in his
honor, that his thoughts turn longingly to
that other way—the strait path leading "To
The Happy Few".

ERIS

86–90 Paul Street   265 Riverside Dr. #4G
London EC2A 4NE   New York, NY 10025

First published in 1903 in the *North American Review*

The moral rights of the author have been asserted.

ISBN 978-1-912475-77-3

eris.press